Mel Bay's

ACTION SONGS
for Children

By Pamela Cooper Bye

Contents

The Crawdad Song

Australia

Arranged by Pamela C. Bye

2. Here comes a man with a pack on his back, Honey.
   Here comes a man with a pack on his back, Babe.
   Here comes a man with a pack on his back,
   Totin' the crawdads in his pack, Honey, Oh Baby mine.

3. Whatcha gonna do when the stream runs dry, Honey.
   Whatcha gonna do when the stream runs dry, Babe.
   Whatcha gonna do when the stream runs dry,
   Sit on the bank, watch the crawdads die, Honey, Oh Baby mine.

Use clapping on beats one and three.

Go Tell Aunt Rhody

Australia

Arranged by Pamela C. Bye

(The) 1. Go tell Aunt Rho - dy, go tell Aunt Rho - dy,

Go tell Aunt Rho - dy, the old grey goose is dead.

2. The one she was saving,
   The one she was saving,
   The one she was saving,
   To make a feather bed.

3. She died in the mill pond,
   She died in the mill pond,
   She died in the mill pond,
   Standing on her head.

Motions

1. On "tell," cup your hands around your mouth.

2. On "to make a feather bed," pat an imaginary bed.

3. On "standing on her head," give this a try if you have some athletic singers, but be careful!

Kookaburra
4 Part Round

Australia

Arranged by Pamela C. Bye

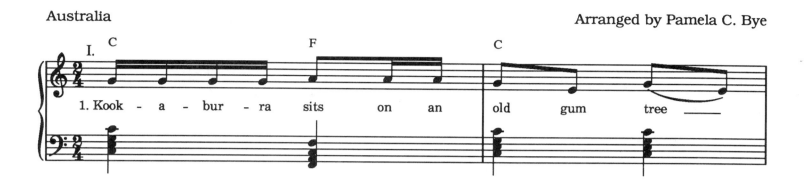

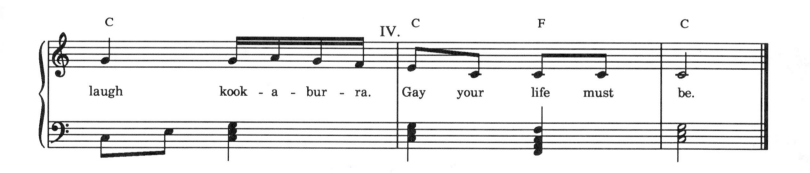

2. Kookaburra sits on the old gum tree,
   Eating all the gum drops he can see.
   Stop! Kookaburra. Stop! Kookaburra,
   Leave some there for me.

There Were Ten in the Bed

Australia

Arranged by Pamela C. Bye

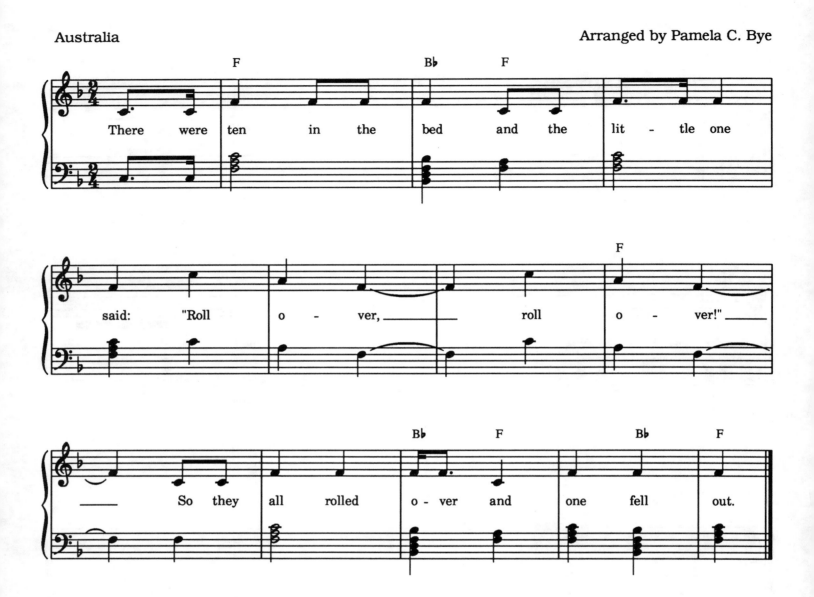

Continue verses: "There were nine in the bed and the little one said," etc.

Last verse. . . and the little one said: "GOOD NIGHT!" (Shouted)

You can do this song with ten children in a row and have *one* person leave the line each time.

Land of The Silver Birch

Canada

Arranged by Pamela C. Bye

Use a simple drum or tom-tom with this song. Divide the group in half and have one half sing the verse while the other sings the chorus.

I'm a Little Teapot

England

Arranged by Pamela C. Bye

Motions

1. Hands over each other
2. Palms facing each other, but far apart
3. Left hand on hip
4. Right elbow on hip hand pointing out for spout
5. Tip over from waist toward the right (spout)

In a Cabin in the Woods

England

Arranged by Pamela C. Bye

Motions

In a cabin in the woods _____	Use hands to make a roof overhead.
Little man by the window stood _____	Hand above eyes as if looking far
Little rabbit hopping by _____	All hop up and down
Knocking at my door. _____	Knock 5 times
"Help me, help me, help," he said, _____	Arms and hands out as if pleading
"'Fore the hunter shoot me dead!" _____	Form imaginary gun and point
"Little rabbit come inside, _____	Motion to come in
Safely you'll abide." _____	Hold rabbit and pet

Children enjoy singing this song and gradually leaving out words until only
the motions are left.

Jim Along Josie

England

Arranged by Pamela C. Bye

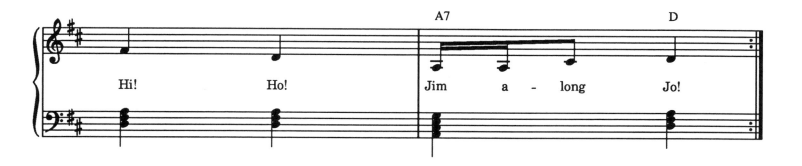

Motions

Hi!_ _ _ _ _ _ _ _ _ _ _ _	Clap twice.
Ho!_ _ _ _ _ _ _ _ _ _ _ _	Slap knees twice.
Jim along_ _ _ _ _ _ _ _	Clap twice.
Josie_ _ _ _ _ _ _ _ _ _	Slap knees twice. . . etc.

This song gets faster and faster.

Little Tommy Tinker

England

Arranged by Pamela C. Bye

Lit - tle Tom Tink - er sat on a clink - er and he be - gan to cry: "Ma! Ma! Poor lit - tle in - no - cent I!"

Motions

1. All stand and sing.
2. All sit.
3. All jump up quickly.
4. Rub eyes with fists.
5. Cup hands around mouth to call.
6. Pat your backsides as if in pain.

London Bridge

England

Arranged by Pamela C. Bye

1. Lon - don Bridge is fall - ing down, fall - ing down, fall - ing down. Lon - don Bridge is fall - ing down, My fair la - dy.

2. Build it up with bricks and stone,
   bricks and stone, bricks and stone.
   Build it up with bricks and stone.
   My fair lady.

Motions

1. Two children form an arch by raising their arms above their heads to make a bridge. The other children skip under the "bridge" while singing.

2. Children circle back under "bridge" in opposite direction until the song is over.

The Noble Duke of York

England

Arranged by Pamela C. Bye

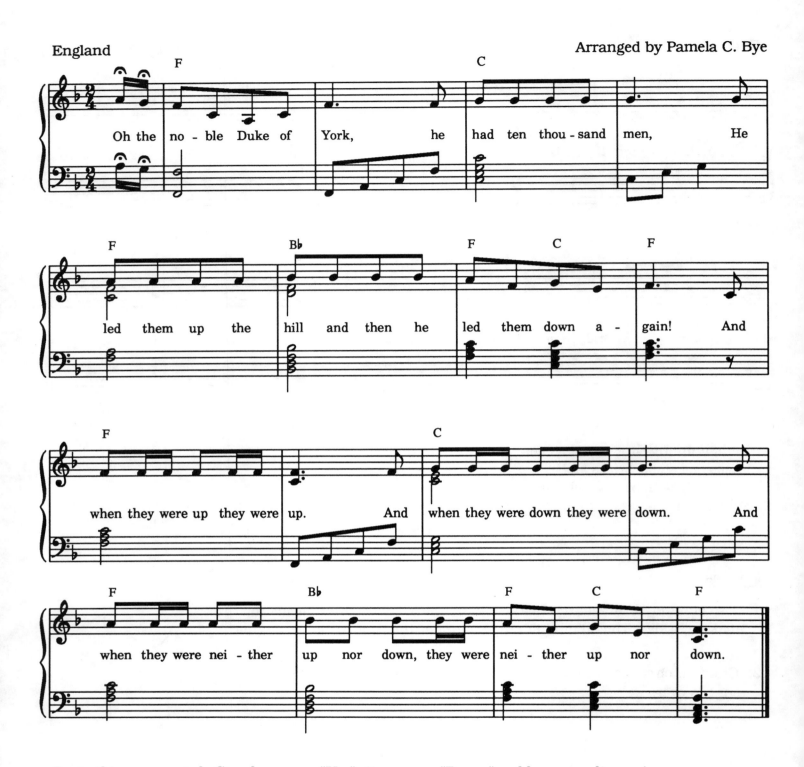

Oh the no - ble Duke of York, he had ten thou - sand men, He led them up the hill and then he led them down a - gain! And when they were up they were up. And when they were down they were down. And when they were nei - ther up nor down, they were nei - ther up nor down.

Begin this song seated. Stand on every "Up," sit on every "Down," and keep speeding up!

Oh, In the Woods

England

Arranged by Pamela C. Bye

This song works well as a leader-group response song, with the children singing the words in parentheses. Other verses may be added, i.e. "And on the tree, there was a limb," etc.

Pussy Cat, Pussy Cat

England

Arranged by Pamela C. Bye

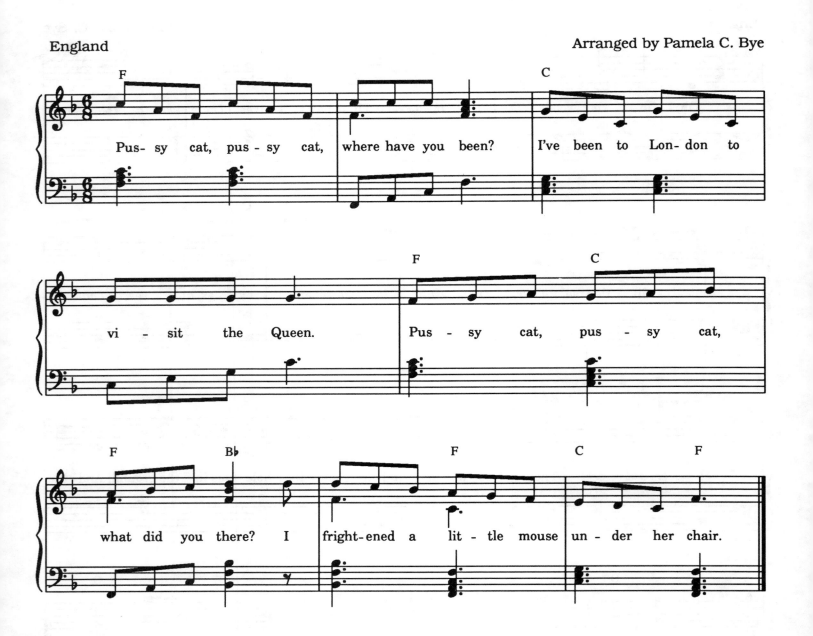

Pus- sy cat, pus- sy cat, where have you been? I've been to Lon- don to vi - sit the Queen. Pus - sy cat, pus - sy cat, what did you there? I fright-ened a lit - tle mouse un - der her chair.

Ride a Cock Horse to Banbury Cross

England

Arranged by Pamela C. Bye

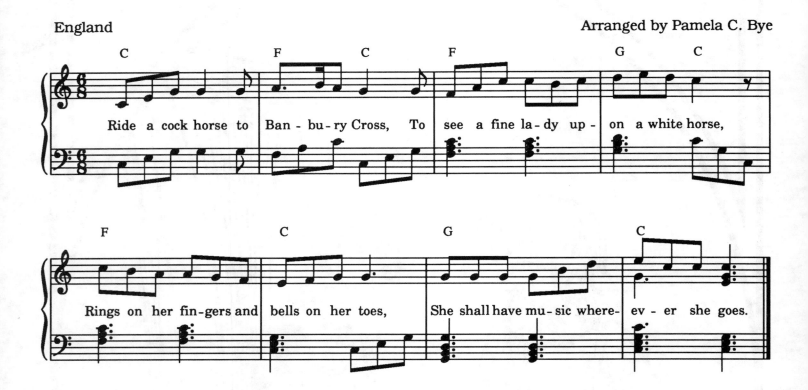

Ride a cock horse to Ban - bu - ry Cross, To see a fine la - dy up - on a white horse,

Rings on her fin - gers and bells on her toes, She shall have mu - sic where- ev - er she goes.

Motions

"Ride . . . Banbury Cross" - hands in front, as holding reins

"Ring . . . fingers" - wiggle fingers

"Bells . . .toes" - wiggle toes

Ring Around a Rosy

England

Arranged by Pamela C. Bye

Ring a ring a ro - sy, Poc - ket full of po - seys.

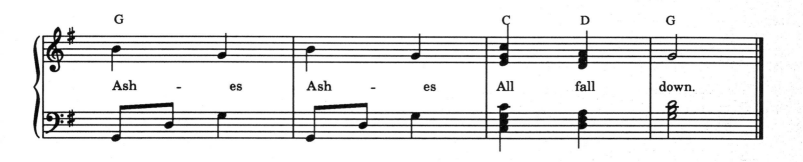

Ash - es Ash - es All fall down.

Motions

Hold hands and circle in a ring while singing -
On "all fall down," drop hands and sit down.

Why Doesn't My Goose?

England

Arranged by Pamela C. Bye

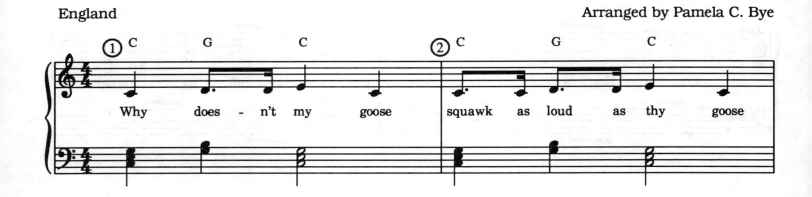

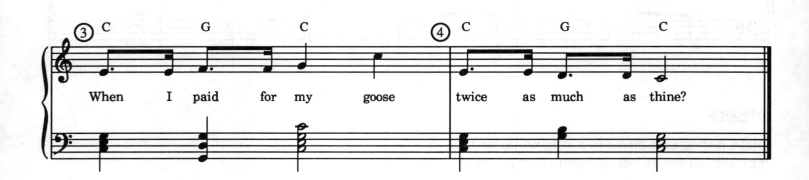

Have the children sing this in a round once all have learned the melody well.

Sing *seated* and select different children to "squawk" at the appropriate time.
The "squawker" jumps up.

Alouette

France

Arranged by Pamela C. Bye

*2. le bec
 3. le cou
 4. les jambes
 5. les pieds
 6. les pattes
} Repeat cumulatively back to "tête"

*This Old Man

Ireland

Arranged by Pamela C. Bye

This old man, he played one, He played nick-nack on my thumb, With a nick-nack pad-dy whack give a dog a bone, This old man came roll-ing home.

Motions

This old man, he played one	Hold up 1 finger.
He played nick-nack on my thumb,	Hold up thumb.
With a nick-nack, paddy-whack, give a dog a bone.	Clap on beat.
This old man came rolling home.	Bend arms in front, and circle hands around each other.

This old man, he played. . .

Two	shoe, etc.	Tap shoe.
Three	knee	Tap knee.
Four	floor	Tap floor.
Five	hive	Tap sides of head.
Six	sticks	Tap index fingers together.
Seven	up in heaven	Fold hands as if praying and point up.
Eight	at my gate	Knock on floor as if asking to come in.
Nine	on my spine	Run thumb up and down spine.
Ten	once again	Open hands to show 10 fingers.

*Everyone should be awake after this one!

My Hat It Has Three Corners

Italy

Arranged by Pamela C. Bye

1st time - Sing as is.
2nd time - On "hat," make pointed cap over head.
3rd time - Hold up 3 fingers every time you sing "three."
4th time - Point elbows up on "corners."

When everyone knows the tune and motions, leave out words when you do the motions.

Everybody Loves Saturday Night

Nigeria

Arranged by Pamela C. Bye

Use clapping! Rhythm instruments would also be effective.

NIGERIAN:	Bobo waro fero Satodeh,
	Bobo waro fero Satodeh,
	Bobo waro, bobo waro,
	Bobo waro fero Satodeh.
FRENCH:	Tout le monde aime Samedi soir.
YIDDISH:	Jeder eyne hot lieb Shabas ba nacht.
CHINESE:	Ren ren si huan li pai lu.
RUSSIAN:	Vsiem nravitsa subbota vietcherom.
CZECH:	Kazhdi ma rad sabotu vietcher.
SPANISH:	A todos les gusta la noche del Sabado.
ITALIAN:	Tutti vogliono il sabato sera.

The Bear Went Over the Mountain

United States

Arranged by Pamela C. Bye

Skip in a circle, stop on "see," and put hand above eyes, as if looking
into the distance. Remind children to listen carefully for "see,"
so there won't be a pile up!

The Ants Came Marching

United States

Arranged by Pamela C. Bye

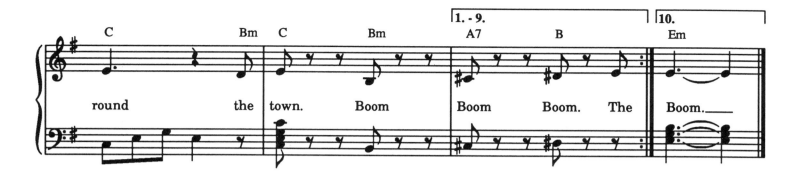

2. The ants came marching two by two. . .
   The little one stopped to tie his shoe. . .

3. The ants came marching three by three. . .
   The little one stopped to climb a tree. . .

4. The ants came marching four by four. . .
   The little one stopped to shut the door. . .

5. The ants came marching five by five. . .
   The little one stopped to take a dive. . .

6. The ants came marching six by six. . .
   The little one stopped to pick up sticks. . .

7. The ants came marching seven by seven. . .
   The little one stopped to go to heaven. . .

8. The ants came marching eight by eight. . .
   The little one stopped to shut the gate. . .

9. The ants came marching nine by nine. . .
   The little one stopped to scratch his spine. . .

10. The ants came marching ten by ten. . .
    The little one stopped to say "THE END!"

Pass out the rhythm instruments and march!

Bingo

United States

Arranged by Pamela C. Bye

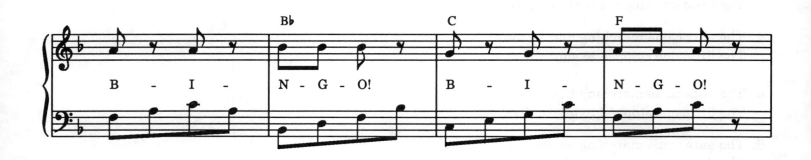

Sing through once as is. Next repetition, leave out "B," and clap instead.

Continue until you are clapping instead of singing on every letter of "BINGO."

Froggie Went A-Courtin'

United States

Arranged by Pamela C. Bye

2. Well, he rode down to Miss Mousie's door, A-huh, A-huh.
   He rode down to Miss Mousie's door, A-huh, A-huh.
   He rode down to Miss Mousie's door,
   Where he had often been before, A-huh, A-huh.

3. He took Miss Mousie on his knee, A-huh, A-huh.
   He took Miss Mousie on his knee, A-huh, A-huh.
   He took Miss Mousie on his knee,
   Said, "Miss Mousie will you marry me?" A-huh, A-huh.

4. "I'll have to ask my Uncle Rat," A-huh, A-huh.
   "I'll have to ask my Uncle Rat," A-huh, A-huh.
   "I'll have to ask my Uncle Rat,"
   "See what he will say to that," A-huh, A-huh.

5. Well, Uncle Rat rode off to town, A-huh, A-huh.
   Uncle Rat rode off to town, A-huh, A-huh.
   Uncle Rat rode off to town,
   To buy his niece a wedding gown, A-huh, A-huh.

6. "Where will the wedding supper be?" A-huh, A-huh.
   "Where will the wedding supper be?" A-huh, A-huh.
   "Where will the wedding supper be?"
   "Way down yonder in a hollow tree," A-huh, A-huh.

7. "What will the wedding supper be?" A-huh, A-huh.
   "What will the wedding supper be?" A-huh, A-huh.
   "What will the wedding supper be?"
   "A friend mosquito and a roasted flea," A-huh, A-huh.

8. First come in were two little ants, A-huh, A-huh.
   First come in were two little ants, A-huh, A-huh.
   First come in were two little ants,
   Fixing around to have a dance, A-huh, A-huh.

9. Next to come in was a bumblebee, A-huh, A-huh.
   Next to come in was a bumblebee, A-huh, A-huh.
   Next to come in was a bumblebee,
   Bouncing a fiddle on his knee, A-huh, A-huh.

10. Next to come in was a big tom cat, A-huh, A-huh.
    Next to come in was a big tom cat, A-huh, A-huh.
    Next to come in was a big tom cat,
    Swallowed the frog and the mouse and the rat, A-huh, A-huh.

11. Next to come in was a big old snake, A-huh, A-huh.
    Next to come in was a big old snake, A-huh, A-huh.
    Next to come in was a big old snake,
    He chased the party into the lake, A-huh, A-huh.

12. That's the end of him and her, A-huh, A-huh.
    That's the end of him and her, A-huh, A-huh.
    That's the end of him and her,
    There'll be no tadpoles covered with fur, A-huh, A-huh.

Go To Sleep Little Baby

United States

Arranged by Pamela C. Bye

Sit in a circle to sing this song, which will help everyone settle down a little.
Simple motions should be used, i.e. fold hands to side and lay head down,
as on a pillow, and clap palms together lightly on "patty cake."

Hush Little Baby

United States

Arranged by Pamela C. Bye

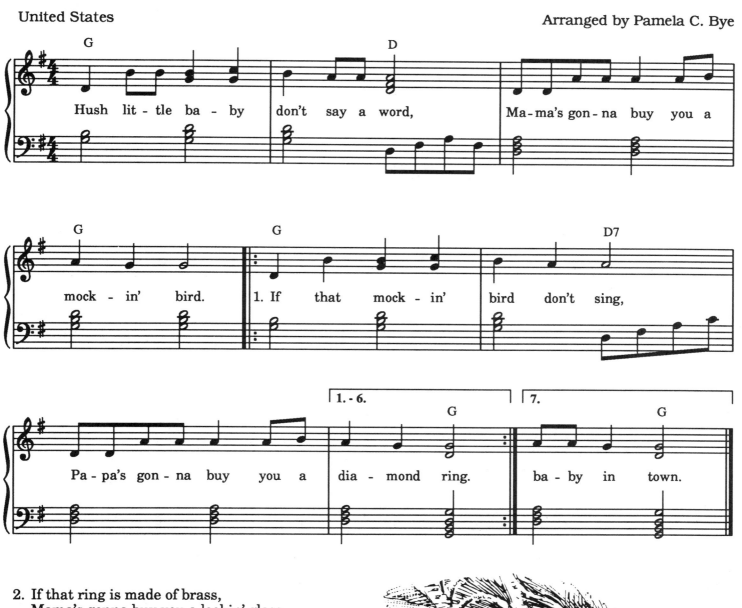

Hush lit - tle ba - by don't say a word, Ma - ma's gon - na buy you a mock - in' bird. 1. If that mock - in' bird don't sing, Pa - pa's gon - na buy you a dia - mond ring. ba - by in town.

2. If that ring is made of brass,
   Mama's gonna buy you a lookin' glass.

3. If that lookin' glass gets broke,
   Papa's gonna buy you a billy goat.

4. If that billy goat don't pull,
   Mama's gonna buy you a cart and bull.

5. If that cart and bull turn over,
   Papa's gonna buy you a dog named Rover.

6. If that dog named Rover don't bark,
   Mama's gonna buy you a horse and cart.

7. If that horse and cart fall down,
   You'll be the sweetest little boy/girl in town.

The Eensy-Weensy Spider

United States

Arranged by Pamela C. Bye

Motions

1. Wiggle fingers while raising arms to simulate spider climbing.
2. Lower arms, wiggle fingers for rain and make a sweeping motion.
3. Both arms over head to form a sun.
4. Same as number one.

I Had a Little Rooster

United States

Arranged by Pamela C. Bye

Have children add other animals and sounds of their own.

I Don't Want To March in The Infantry

United States

Arranged by Pamela C. Bye

Motions

"March" _ _ _ _ _ _ _ _ _ _ _ _ _ _ _ March in place.

"Shoot" _ _ _ _ _ _ _ _ _ _ _ _ _ _ Aim imaginary gun.

"Ride" _ _ _ _ _ _ _ _ _ _ _ _ _ _ _ Hold reins.

"Sail" _ _ _ _ _ _ _ _ _ _ _ _ _ _ _ Hands make side to side motion.

"I just wanna be friends" _ _ _ Wave to someone.

Monkey See, Monkey Do

United States

Arranged by Pamela C. Bye

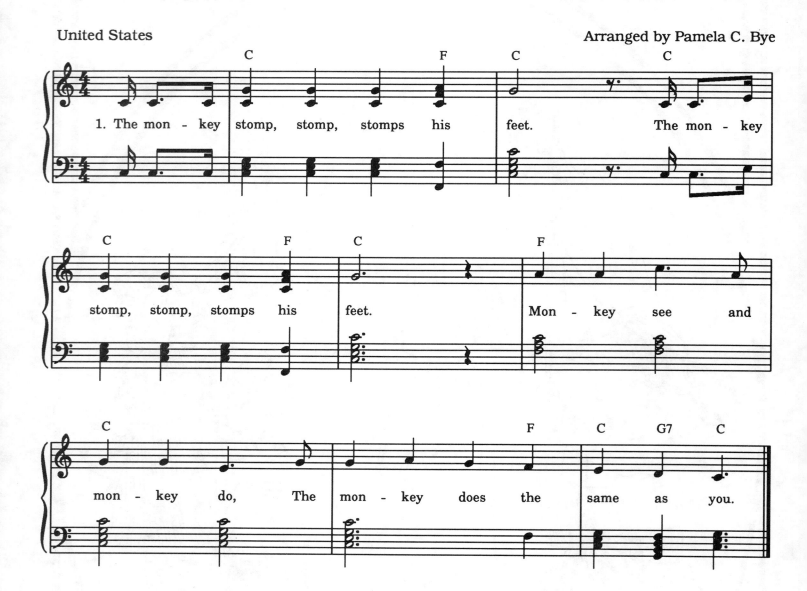

2. The monkey clap, clap, claps his hands.
   The monkey clap, clap, claps his hands.
   Monkey see and monkey do,
   The monkey does the same as you.

Motions

Vs. 1 - Stomp the feet.
Vs. 2- Clap hands.

This is a good song for having the children make up verses of their own.

The Muffin Man

United States

Arranged by Pamela C. Bye

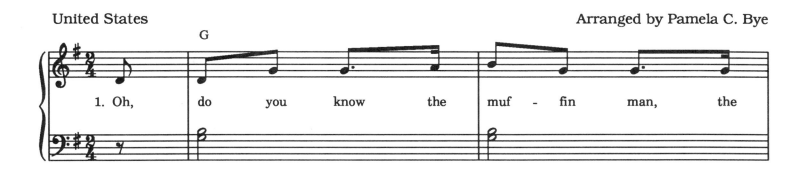

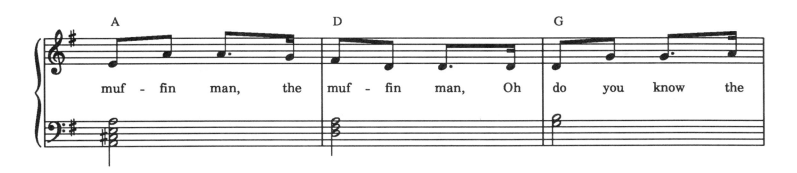

2. Oh, yes I know the muffin man
   the muffin man, the muffin man,
   Oh, yes I know the muffin man
   who lives across the way.

The teacher can point to someone, and his name can be substituted,
i.e. "Charlie is the muffin man. . .

New River Train

United States/Africa

Arranged by Pamela C. Bye

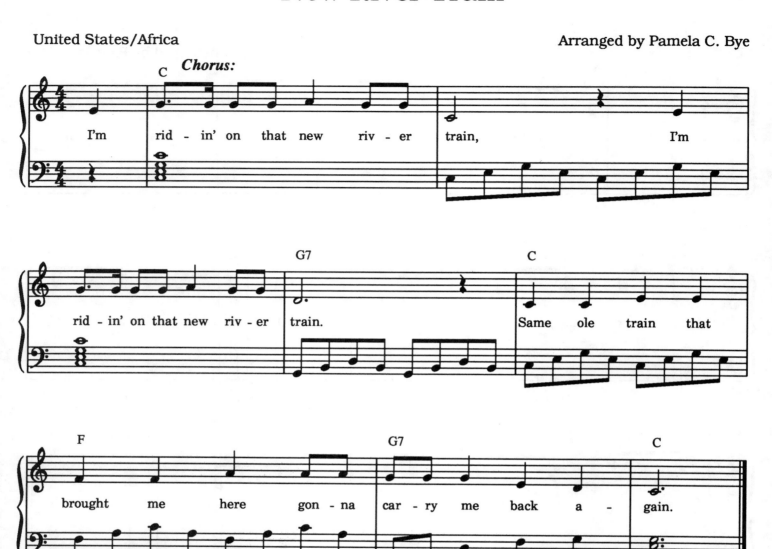

Chorus:

I'm rid - in' on that new riv - er train, I'm
rid - in' on that new riv - er train. Same ole train that
brought me here gon - na car - ry me back a - gain.

Younger children could form a train and move around the room, speeding up and slowing down.

Oh Where Has My Little Dog Gone?

United States

Arranged by Pamela C. Bye

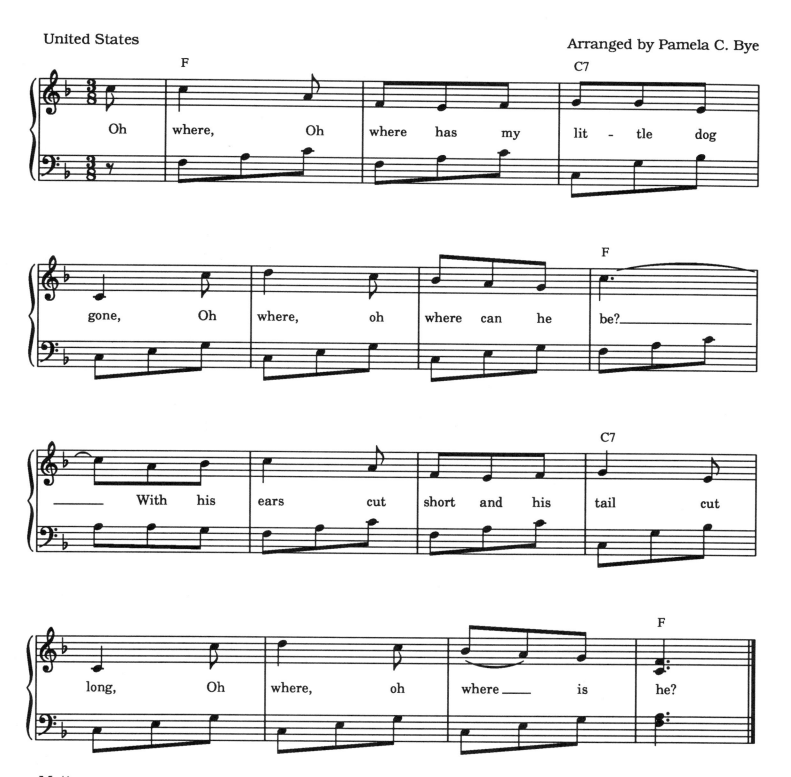

Motions

"Oh, where". . . Hands in front, palms up as if questioning

". . .ears cut short" . . . Use hands to cup behind ears

". . .tail cut long". . . Hands far apart to show long tail

Old MacDonald Had a Farm

United States

Arranged by Pamela C. Bye

2. . . . had some ducks. . . . .quack, quack here, etc.
3. . . . had some cows. . . . . .moo, moo here, etc.
4. . . . had some pigs. . . . . . oink, oink here, etc.
5. . . . had some sheep. . . . .baa, baa, here etc.

Have the children add other animals, and make the most of the animal
sounds in the verses.

One Finger, One Thumb, One Hand

United States

Arranged by Pamela C. Bye

2. One ankle, one foot, one toe, one knee, keep moving.
   Repeat
   Repeat
   And we'll all be happy today.

Motions - vs. 1 & 2

Point to various body parts as they are mentioned, or use that body part.
Clap where the Xs are shown.

Six Little Ducks

United States

Arranged by Pamela C. Bye

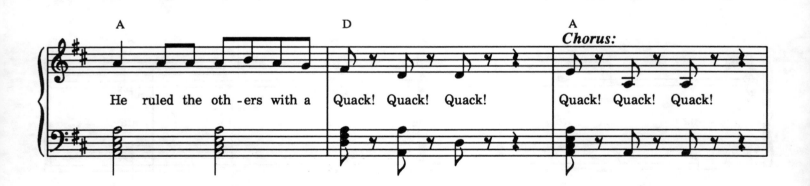

Motions

1. Six little ducks that I once knew _ _ _ _ _ _ _ _ _ _ _ _ _ _ Hold up 6 fingers,
   fat ones, skinny one, tall ones too   Arms far apart,
                                                Arms close together,
                                                Hands above one another.

   But the one little duck with the, _ _ _ _ _ _ _ _ _ _ _ _ _ _ Hands behind back,
   feathers on his back,   fingers wiggling.

   He ruled the others with a Quack, _ _ _ _ _ _ _ _ _ _ _ _ _ Tuck hands under arms
   Quack, Quack   and move elbows up and
                                                down for wings, or for
                                                each Quack.

2. Down to the river they would go _ _ _ _ _ _ _ _ _ _ _ _ _ _ Point Down.
   Wibble, wabble, wibble, wabble to and fro   Tuck hands under
                                                and waddle in a circle.

   Home from the river they would come, _ _ _ _ _ _ _ _ _ _ Motion "come here."

   Wibble, wabble, wibble, wabble _ _ _ _ _ _ _ _ _ _ _ _ _ _ _ Imitate ducks again-
   Ho-hum-hum.   yawn and cover mouth
                                                on "Ho-hum-hum."

Three Little Kittens

United States

Arranged by Pamela C. Bye

2. The three little kittens, they found their mittens,
   And they began to cry,
   "Oh, mother dear, see here, see here!
   Our mittens we have found!"
   "What! Found your mittens?
   You darling kittens!
   Then you shall have some pie."
   "Meow, meow, meow, meow!"

3. The three little kittens put on their mittens,
   And soon ate up the pie.
   "Oh, mother dear, we greatly fear
   Our mittens we have soiled."
   "What! Soiled your mittens?
   You naughty kittens."
   They they began to sing,
   "Meow, meow, meow, meow!"

4. The three little kittens, they washed their mittens,
   And hung them up to dry.
   "Oh, mother dear, look here, look here!
   Our mittens we have washed."
   "What! Washed your mittens?
   You darling kittens!
   But I smell a rat close by!
   "Hush, hush, hush, hush!"

Motions

"Mittens" - Every time, hold hands in front and wiggle from the wrist.

"Cry"   - Rub eyes with fists.

"Meow"   - Really meow.

This song can be divided into parts and used as a playlet: 3 kittens
                                                              Mama
                                                              Rat

Pop! Goes the Weasel

United States

Arranged by Pamela C. Bye

Sing seated and jump up on "Pop" each time.

The Wheels On The Bus

United States

Arranged by Pamela C. Bye

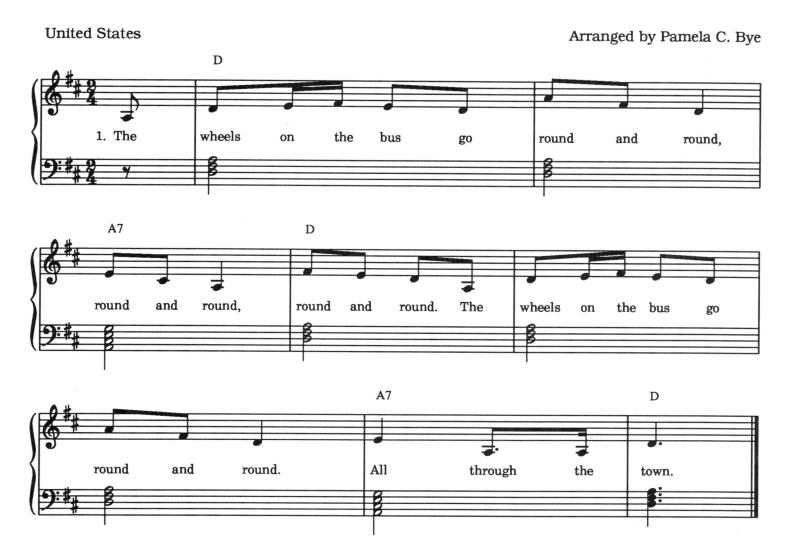

2. The money in the box goes 'Clink, clink, clink,". . .

3. The wipers on the bus go "Swish, swish, swish.". . .

4. The horn on the bus goes "Beep, beep, beep,". . .

Motions for vs. 1-4

1. Fold arms and make a rolling motion.

2. Clap on "Clink, clink, clink."

3. Move arms back and forth from elbows like wipers.

4. Cup hands around mouth on "Beep, beep, beep."

Other Suggestions:

Have the children make up verses of their own.
Use rhythm instruments. . . ie. triangle on verse 2.

Where Is Thumbkin?

United States

Arranged by Pamela C. Bye

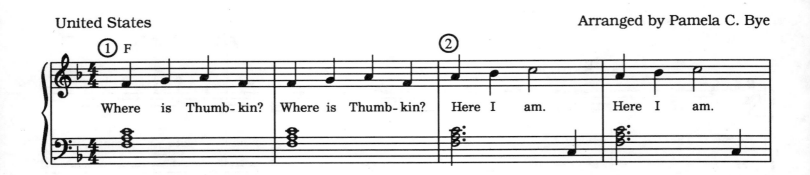

Motions

1. Hands behind back.

2. One hand in front with thumb up, followed immediately by other hand thumb up.

3. Wiggle right thumb, answer by wiggling left thumb.

4. Right hand behind back, followed by left hand.

A-Tisket-A-Tasket

Traditional

Arranged by Pamela C. Bye

Stand in a circle holding hands. One person holding a handkerchief skips around the outside, and on "dropped," drops the handkerchief behind someone. That person picks it up and chases the "dropper," who is trying to claim that person's place in the circle. The song begins again with the new "dropper."

Arr. Copyright © 1992 by Mel Bay Publications, Inc., Pacific, MO 63069.
International copyright secured. All rights reserved.

Baa! Baa! Black Sheep

Traditional

Arranged by Pamela C. Bye

Divide the class into two groups:
One side sings "Baa. . . wool?" Other side answers "Yes, sir. . . full."

On "one," hold up one finger. Switch groups and repeat.

The Farmer In The Dell

Traditional

Arranged by Pamela C. Bye

2. The farmer takes a wife, etc.
3. The wife takes the child, etc.
4. The child takes the nurse, etc.
5. The nurse takes the dog, etc.
6. The dog takes the cat, etc.
7. The cat takes the rat, etc.
8. The rat takes the cheese, etc.
9. The cheese stands alone, etc.

A child representing the farmer stands in the middle of the
circle and chooses a wife at the end of verse 2. The wife chooses
a child, and so on, until the cheese is selected. Then the game
begins over.

I Love Little Kitty

Traditional

Arranged by Pamela C. Bye

I— love lit - tle Kit - ty her coat is so warm, And—
if I don't hurt her she'll do me no harm. I'll sit by the fire — and
give her some food. And— kit - ty will love me be - cause I'm so good.

Claude the Cat

Claude the cat is big and fat,
Ice cream makes him look like that.
Strawberry and chocolate, too.
Any kind will do.

Little Boy Blue

Traditional

Arranged by Pamela C. Bye

Lit - tle Boy Blue, come blow__ your horn, the sheep's in the mea-dow, the cow's in the corn.

Where is the boy who looks af - ter the sheep? He lies in the hay - stack fast a - sleep.

Motions

"Blow your horn" - both hands up in front, as if playing a trumpet

"Where . . ." - hands out, palms *up*, as if questioning

"fast asleep" - hands together to form a pillow

Mary Had a Little Lamb

Traditional

Arranged by Pamela C. Bye

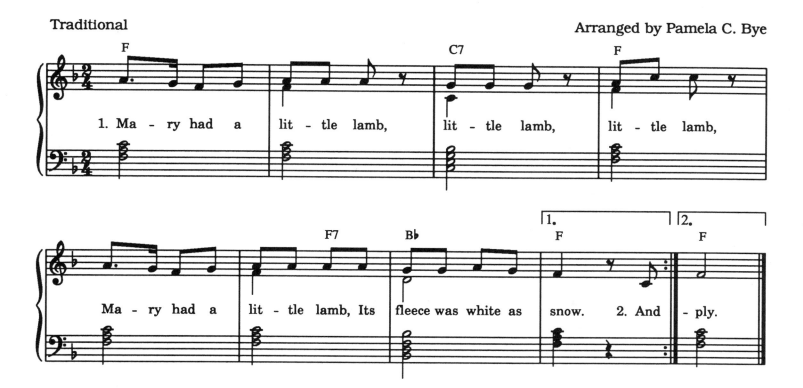

2. And everywhere that Mary went, Mary went, Mary went,
   Everywhere that Mary went the lamb was sure to go!

3. It followed her to school one day, school one day, school one day.
   It followed her to school one day, which was against the rule.

4. It made the children laugh and play, laugh and play, laugh and play.
   It made the children laugh and play to see a lamb at school.

5. And so the teacher turned it out, turned it out, turned it out.
   And so the teacher turned it out, but still it lingered near.

6. And waited patiently about, 'ly about, 'ly about, 'ly about.
   And waited patiently about till Mary did appear.

7. Why does the lamb love Mary so, Mary so, Mary so?
   Why does the lamb love Mary so? The eager children cry.

8. Why Mary loves the lamb, you know, lamb, you know, lamb, you know.
   Why Mary loves the lamb, you know, the teacher did reply.

You could have children act the parts of Mary, the lamb, and the teacher.

The Old Gray Mare

Traditional

Arranged by Pamela C. Bye

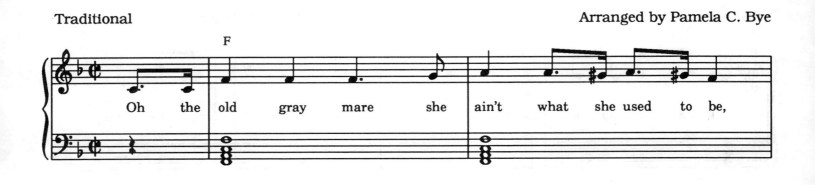

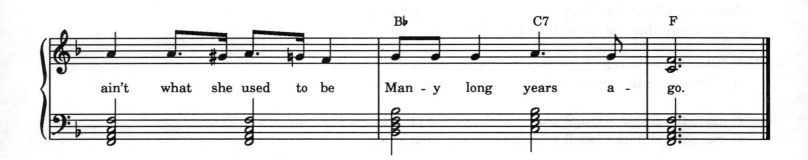

"Ain't what. . . be" - Shake head vigorously back and forth.

Pat-A-Cake

Traditional

Arranged by Pamela C. Bye

"Pat-a-cake . . . fast as you can" - Clap hands together.

"Roll it" - Rolls hands, palms together.

"Mark . . . T" - Draw a T in the air.

"And . . . baby and me" - Rub tummy.

Paw Paw Patch

Traditional

Arranged by Pamela C. Bye

2. Pickin' up paw paws, puttin' 'em in your pocket,
   Pickin' up paw paws, puttin' 'em in your pocket,
   Pickin' up paw paws, puttin' 'em in your pocket,
   Way down yonder in the paw paw patch.

This song is good to use holding hands moving in a circle.
All bend to "pick up paw paws" at the end.

Simple Simon

Traditional

Arranged by Pamela C. Bye

1. Sim - ple Si - mon met a pie man Go - ing to the fair; Said

Sim - ple Si - mon to the pie man, "Let me taste your ware."

2. Said the man to Simple Simon,
   "Show me first your penny."
   Said Simple Simon to the pie man,
   "Rats, I have not any."

Three Blind Mice

Traditional

Arranged by Pamela C. Bye

"Three blind mice" . . . . . Cover eyes with both hands.
"See how they run" . . . . . Scamper around in a circle.
"She cut off their tails" . . Chopping motion with hand.
"Three blind mice" . . . . . Same as before.

Flying Friends

Pamela C. Bye

Pamela C. Bye

2. Lightning bug, lightning bug,
   Blink your light for all to see.
   Lightning bug, lightning bug,
   Make me go "hee, hee."

3. Bumblebee, bumblebee,
   Zoom around and go "buzz, buzz."
   Bumblebee, bumblebee.
   Buzz up to the sky.

4. Butterfly, lightning bug,
   Bumblebee that goes "buzz, buzz."
   Buzz up high, light the sky,
   Fly and give us joy.

Motions

1. Cross hands to indicate wings. Gradually move arms up and down on "Fly up to the sky."

2. Clap once on each syllable; blink eyes on line 2. Clap on line 3. Wrap arms around self and shake as if laughing.

3. Bend over arms straight out to side and move in small circles, like a little plane. Flap arms and put lots of "z" on buzz.

4. Use motions for each creature from the other verses. Flap "wings" for last two lines.

The Garden Song

L. Dean Bye

Pamela C. Bye

Motions

1. Use a digging motion.

2. Move arm from side to side, as if spreading seed.

3. Make a large circle with arms to represent the sun.
   Lower arms slowly, wiggling fingers for rain.

4. Begin with arms lowered, hands pointing to ground, and gradually raise until pointing straight up, on "trees."

Here Comes The Band

Pamela C. Bye

Pamela C. Bye

2. Clang the cymbals, clang them hard.
   Ring out the song for all to hear.
   Clang the cymbals, clang them hard.
   Clang cymbals, clang out loud.

3. Blow the trumpet, loud and strong.
   Toot toot toot toot toot, toot toot toot.
   Blow the trumpet, loud and strong.
   Ta Ta Ta, Ta Ta Ta.

This is a good song for marching, which children love to do. If possible, a small drum
should be used on Vs. 1 and a triangle and bar, or small cymbals should be used on Vs. 2.
Vs. 3 should just be sung because the children will enjoy saying "toot" and "ta."

Our Friends

L. Dean Bye

L. Dean Bye

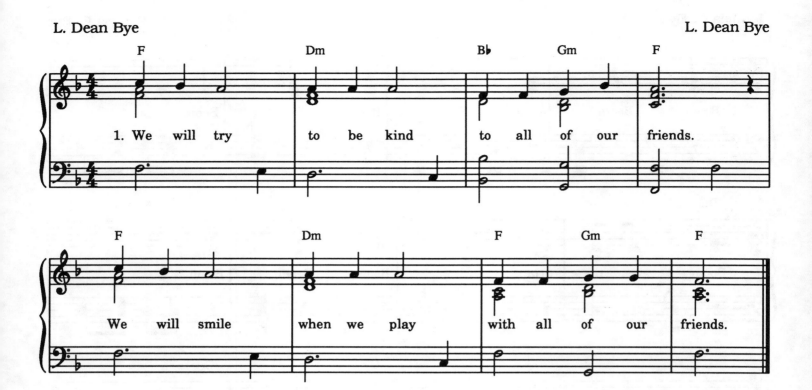

2. We will share all our toys.
   With each of our friends.
   Run and play, laugh and sing.
   With all of our friends.

Motions

1. All hold hands.
2. Turn toward each other, run in place, all hold hands to end.

Thunderstorm

Pamela C. Bye

Pamela C. Bye

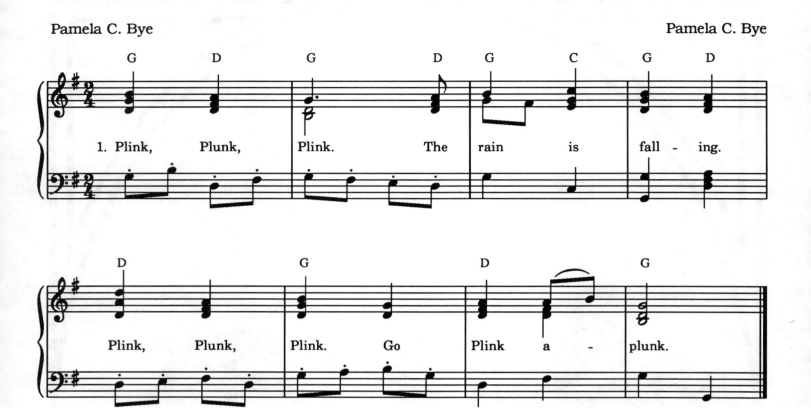

1. Plink, Plunk, Plink. The rain is fall - ing.
Plink, Plunk, Plink. Go Plink a - plunk.

2. Boom, boom, boom.
The thunder rumbles.
Boom, boom, boom
Boom all around.

3. Ooh, ooh, ooh.
The wind is blowing.
Blowing branches,
To and fro.

Motions

1. "Plink" and "Plunk"   - Clap.
   "Rain is falling"   - Arms up, lower while wiggling fingers.

2. "Boom"   - Stomp on one foot, then the other.
   "Thunder rumbles"   - Arms out to side, shake hands.
   "All around"   - Arms together in front, extend to make circle.

3. Arms straight overhead, sway from side to side.